# 7 FACTS WHY JESUS DIDN'T SAY HE WOULD BUILD A CHURCH
## *...and what it means to you*

PUBLISHED BY
KINGDOM WORD PUBLICATIONS
ALBION, MICHIGAN 49224
Printed in the U.S,A

# 7 Facts Why Jesus Didn't Say He Would Build A Church

## ...and what it means to you

ISBN  978-0-9988952-5-3

Library of Congress Control Number:  2018956707

KINGDOM WORD PUBLICATIONS is the publishing division of THE EKKLESIA CENTER The mission of Kingdom Word Publications is to produce and distribute quality books and training materials to strengthen believers who are gathering from house to house, according to the values and structure of first century Christianity.

For more information, visit our website www.TheEkklesiaCenter.org

# TABLE OF CONTENTS

# INTRODUCTION

I can pretty much guarantee that if you opened your bible right now to Matthew 16:18 the text would generally read like this:

> And I say also unto thee, That thou art Peter, and upon this rock I will build my church; and the gates of hell shall not prevail against it. (Matthew 16:18)

Unless you own one of a very few select translations, your bible and mine also records Jesus as saying He would build His church. For me to suggest that He did not say this appears to be silly at best, and heretical at worse. But that is exactly my assertion. Jesus did not say He would build a church. The goal of this book is to prove this fact.

If Jesus did not say He would build a church, it begs the question, "What did He say He would build?" The answer to this implies that whatever He said may be totally different from what we have known.

This opens up another barrage of questions. "If Jesus didn't say He would build a church, what did Jesus actually say?" "Does what He said make a difference?" "If Jesus said something different from what is in our bibles, why was it changed?" These questions should alert you to what you will learn in this book.

You will read a lot about a Greek word ekklesia – pronounced eh-klay-see-ah. You may be among those who have never heard this word. Therefore this book is written to give you the basics as well as the importance of understanding it. You may be among those who are familiar with ekklesia. You may have learned its basic definition of being 'called out'. You may have been taught that it is the Greek word that is translated as church. For you, this book will take you deeper into understanding its history and entomology.

Like most Christians, the word and concept of church is all you have ever known. There has been no reason to question whether there was an issue with defining it. If this book can show you that Jesus never said he would build a church, it will also show you the effect that the 'church mindset' has had on you. If you agree with what you read, my final goal will be to show you what you can do to obey the words of Jesus Christ. It is not enough to simply learn something new. It is important that we implement what we know in our daily walk in the Lord.

As you read, take notes and pray. Then do your own research. I believe the facts are clear. Jesus did not say He would build a church. The impact of this has gone unnoticed, primarily because we didn't know there was a problem. God has greatness planned for you. Learning, and walking in His divine intent will set you free and empower you. Get ready to learn why Jesus never said He would build a church...

Let's get started.

# FACT I: THE ENGLISH WORD CHURCH DID NOT EXIST IN THE FIRST CENTURY

Let's think about the impact of words. I am a child of the 1950's. I have witnessed many new words that have been born out of the advances made in science, technology, education, music, the arts and more.

When I was growing up, our playtime consisted of cowboys and Indians, pretending to be soldiers, superheroes, and riding bikes with balloons in the spokes so they would sound like motorcycles. The most 'techie' type toy we had were a set of walkie-talkies that had a range of about 25 feet. We would hide behind trees, or on opposite sides of our house, just so we could not see each other while we communicated.

It dawned on me recently how different the world is for my children, grandchildren and great-grandchildren. They live in a world quite different from my childhood days. Their gadgets include iPads, iPods, Laptops, and cell phones.

Concepts like texting, email, skype, Facetime, and on-line chatting were unheard of. Technology using megabytes, gigabytes and terabytes seemed light years away from my Etch-A-Sketch era.

Communication systems like Facebook, Instagram, Messenger, Snapchat, Twitter, and the like would have been relegated to sci-fi programs like Lost in Space, Captain Z-ro, Batman and Space Patrol. Yet, each of the technological equipment I mentioned, as well as the phrases and systems that accompany them are a normal part of our lives today.

Back then, we communicated by telephone and with pen and pencil. Today, not only is texting the communication method of choice, but it too has spawned new ways of expressing your thoughts. In my day, if I were to write LOL, SMH, HMU and TBT, these would have been considered misspelled words. If I had dared to say out loud what LMBO meant, my parents or any adult who heard me say it would have smacked me on the mouth.

## The words we understand today reflect the both the culture and environment of our society

Words paint pictures in our mind. For example, when I say that someone texted me, you immediately without conscious effort, get a picture in your mind of someone with a small digital device thumbing away at a miniature keyboard to relay the message they want to send me. The word texting paints a picture, and you know clearly what I mean.

I share this to make a critical point. The words we understand to-day reflect both the culture and environment of our society. I suspect there will be new words that will crop up as society continues to evolve. The fact is, there are words we use today that did not exist when I was a child.

## WORDS IN THE FIRST CENTURY

The world Jesus lived in had words that reflected the culture and environment of that era. They too painted pictures in the minds of the hearer.

Jesus Christ was – and is – a master communicator. His words are clear and penetrating. Even His strategic use of parables hit their target in the hearts of those to whom their message was intended.

> Therefore speak I to them in parables: because they seeing see not; and hearing they hear not, neither do they understand. And in them is fulfilled the prophecy of Esaias, which saith, By hearing ye shall hear, and shall not understand; and seeing ye shall see, and shall not perceive: (Matthew 13:13-14)

Jesus was also at times demonstrative when he wanted to make a specific point. When a young lady was caught in adultery, He slowly wrote something in the sand and then gave any accuser of the woman the opportunity to be the first to carry out the law and stone her. Of course, to qualify, they had to be without sin. You know the outcome of that story.

> They said this testing him, that they might have something to accuse him of. But Jesus stooped down, and wrote on the ground with his finger. But when

they continued asking him, he looked up and said to them, "He who is without sin among you, let him throw the first stone at her." Again he stooped down, and with his finger wrote on the ground. They, when they heard it, being convicted by their conscience, went out one by one, beginning from the oldest, even to the last. Jesus was left alone with the woman where she was, in the middle. Jesus, standing up, saw her and said, "Woman, where are your accusers? Did no one condemn you?" She said, "No one, Lord." Jesus said, "Neither do I condemn you. Go your way. From now on, sin no more." (John 8:6-11 *World English Bible*)

In another incident, a blind man was brought to Him to be healed. Rather than heal Him on the spot as He had done before many other times, He led the man outside of the city and used dirt mixed with His saliva to heal him. I believe Jesus was making a not so subtle statement to the city, which happened to be Bethsaida; a city that He had upbraided because of their rejection of the wonderful works of God (Matthew 11:21; Mark 8:22-26).

Soon after this, Jesus led His young disciples to a dark and demonic place called Caesarea Philippi. There they would see the images of dead Caesars carved into the mountainside. They would see the temple of the goat god Pan, where vulgar sexual acts were taking place in the open. They would see a cave with a river flowing through it where both human and animal sacrifices were common. This cave was commonly known as the Gate of Hades.

It was in this foreboding place where Jesus asked His young followers what people were saying about Him. From their first responses, it appeared that most people had concluded that Jesus was a reincarnation of Jeremiah, Elijah, John the Baptist or some of the prophets who were dead.

But this same question to His disciples moves us closer to the point we are making in this book, that Jesus never said He would build a church. Peter exclaimed, "You are the Christ, Son of the Living God!" This revelatory response, prompted by God Himself, seemed to satisfy Jesus. What Peter said became the basis of what He declared He would build.

Let's step back for a moment. Everything that Caesarea Philippi represented was known to the disciples. Whether they had been there or not, the repu-

> ...'church', is an English word that did not exist in the first century

tation of the area would have been familiar to them. Jesus said the gate of Hades would not prevail over what He would build. The disciples were literally looking at the cave bearing that name.

WHAT EXACTLY DID JESUS SAY HE WOULD BUILD?

Most bibles say that He would build His church. However, there is a problem with this.

First, Jesus was most likely speaking in Greek, or Aramaic. Second, His choice of words would have been familiar to His disciples. And third, the word 'church', is an English word that did not exist in the first century. Stop. I repeat, the English word church did not exist in the first century.

If Jesus had said He would build a church, the disciples would have had no clue – by definition or concept – as to what He was talking about.

What did Jesus actually say?

Jesus said He would build His ekklesia, pronounced *eh klay see ah*. The Greek word for church is *kurikon*. These are two entirely different words. The word 'church' finds its beginning around the fourth or fifth centuries, several hundred years after Jesus Christ walked the earth.

Interestingly the word church was more common among the pagans. Early pagans used the Greek words *kuriakê oikia* to reference a building belonging to the lord or the lord's house. The image of a building is the most common image we have of church today.

In our English translation of kuriakê oikia, we have not capitalized the word 'lord'. This is because there is some serious questions as to which 'lord' was being referenced. The "lord's house" used by pagans in the 4th century clearly did not refer to the Lord Jesus Christ, but rather to the sun-god Mithra.

Mithra was a famous god among the pagans but with many different names. It was Constantine, who worshipped Mithra as his god. He brought the pagan god Mithra into Christianity. Christian worship became a state sanctioned religion. It left the simplicity of gathering from house to house, and adherents started meeting in dedicated temples similar to those used by the pagans. He transformed the called-out assembly into the concept of church which became more recognized by a building – just as it is today. He also set his appointed clergy in charge of the house.[1]

In 1524, William Tyndale published the first English bible. He translated ekklesia as 'congregation'. This is a much better, but not a perfect translation. Other translations that followed such as The Bishops Bible and the Geneva Bible followed the lead of Tyndale's version.

The first edition of the Webster's dictionary in 1828, revealed the pagan roots of the word church even further. In it, the first entry as to the etymology of church is 'circe' (pronounced seer see).

Circe can be traced back to Greek mythology. Circe was purportedly a Greek goddess. She was alleged to be the daughter of the Sun God Helios and Perse. She was believed to have great knowledge of magic and venomous herbs who turned her victims into wild animals. It is the same word, or name Circe that in time was translated into the word church.

There are other words like chirche, kirk, kerk, and kirche that have Anglo-Saxon, Scottish, German and Norrish roots that also were translated as church. Each of these evolved many years after Jesus Christ and the disciples were at Caesarea Philippi.

So, what does this all mean? The first reason Jesus did not say He would build a church is due to the etymological and historic fact that

---

[1]https://www.therealchurch.com/articles/the_word_that_changed_the_world.html

7

the word 'church' did not exist during Jesus lifetime. Second, if it did, the pagan roots of the word church would not make sense for Jesus to use — especially at Caesarea Philippi.

One hundred and fifteen times in our bibles, there is the word church. It was never used by Jesus, nor the original writers of New Testament text. Every time the original language used ekklesia. This leads us to the next fact showing why Jesus never said He would build a Church.

# FACT 2: EKKLESIA WAS PURPOSELY MISTRANSLATED AS CHURCH

In the first chapter of this book you learned that the word church did not exist in Jesus' day. You also learned that it has deep pagan roots. This makes it very unlikely that if the word church had been around in Jesus time, He most likely would not have used it as something He would build. So how did church become such a common word for us today?

In my book, LEAVING CHURCH BECOMING EKKLESIA, the entire fourth chapter of the book delves into this question. That chapter, HOW EKKLESIA BECAME CHURCH, can be accessed in its entirety on our website www.TheEC.org, under the Free Resources section. In this book I will summarize that chapter.

Nearly any translation of the bible you choose, Matthew 16:18 will record Jesus as declaring that He would *build His 'church'*. I have checked and continue to check many translations and have found two that used the word *assembly* instead of *church*. The World English

Bible Translation, and The Emphasized New Testament[1] do not use the word church. There may be a few more, but the great majority of bible translations use *church*.

The original Greek word for church, kyriakon is not the word that Jesus used. He said He would build His ekklesia. Simply put, ekklesia is not church. Clearly there is an error in the translation.

Mistakes happen, and our understanding of words evolve over time. For example, today when we use the word enthusiasm, we are referring to a level of excitement exhibited by an individual. We want people to be enthusiastic about what they do. However, when the word enthusiasm was originally used, specifically by the Puritans, it had a derogatory sense. They used it to describe someone who had excessive religious emotion. The root word itself means to be divinely inspired, generally by God or a god. Today, many other adjectives are applied to the word enthusiasm. You can be a camping enthusiast, a biking enthusiast, a jazz enthusiast, and yes, some may be considered a 'church' enthusiasts. None of these are usually stated in a negative or derogatory sense.

> ...ekklesia was deliberately mistranslated by the authority of King James

Let's be honest, most of the time you hear the word church spoken by a believer, it is in a positive framework. Regardless of its pagan origins, people revere and admire their church. Church as a word, has evolved into a positive word generally associated with Christianity.

---

[1] Kregel Publications. *The Emphasized New Testament* by Joseph Bryant Rotherham.

The facts show us that church is not the proper translation of ekklesia. How did this happen? Was this a literary mistake? Is it just a matter of words evolving over time, as some have suggested? The answer to this is another fact that reveals why Jesus never said He would build a church.

## A WILLFUL MISTRANSLATION

The word ekklesia was deliberately mistranslated by the authority of King James. Let that sink in for a moment. The switch from ekklesia to church, was done on purpose. It was not an accident. Ekklesia is the original word that Jesus spoke, and it should have been kept. At the very least it should have been translated as an assembly or congregation, but King James appeared to want every hint of its true meaning erased. Why?

> …[King James] specifically told them to use the word *church* instead of the correct translation of *ekklesia – assembly or congregation…*

To understand the reason behind this change, let's consider some historical facts about King James. From his own writings, he considered himself a god. For example, during a dispute over the marriage of one of his sons, he disbanded the parliament for their criticisms. He is quoted as saying,

> "Monarchy is the greatest thing on earth. _Kings are rightly called gods_ since just like God they have power of life and death over all their subjects in all things. They are accountable to God only ... _so it is a crime for anyone to argue about what a king can do_."[2]

---

[2] http://www.greatsite.com/timeline-english-bible-history/king-james.html

This statement coincides with his publishing of two books, *The Divine Right of Kings* and *The True Law of Free Monarchies*. Both show the absolute godlike authority he felt he, and all kings had. His line of thinking was demonstrated when the Puritans attempted to challenge the hierarchal order of the Church of England. They had proposed the use of a presbytery, along with the bishops. King James angrily rebuked them. He saw this as an attempt to diminish his power in the church.[3] Remember, he felt as king that he had absolute power. His mindset is important to understand in relationship to the *ekklesia*.

King James was well educated. Some historians say that he was more of a scholar than warrior. He understood the original languages of scripture, and the word ekklesia, and its implications, most likely, did not escape him.

Remember there were English translations of the bible before the King James Version. The Tyndale bible was the first known of these, and in it, ekklesia was translated as congregation.

> And I saye also vnto the yt thou arte Peter: and apon this rocke I wyll bylde my congregacion. And the gates of hell shall not prevayle ageynst it. (Matthew 16:18 Original Tyndale Version)

There were subsequent English translations including the General Bible, the Bishop's Bible and the Geneva Bible. These translations are considered amplifications of Tyndale's original work since the bulk of their content was shaped by his.

In his book, Ekklesia: Rediscovering God's Instrument for Global Transformation, Dr. Ed Silvoso wrote:

---

[3] King James favored the system where the he could rule the church through bishops

King James, however, was displeased with those translations being available to common folks, in particular the Geneva Bible's Explanatory Notes...

...The teaching those Notes contained on church government ran diametrically counter to his belief in the "divine right of kings," which ascribes absolute power to sovereigns to rule uncontested in every area of their reign.

The king convened 47 scholars to produce a new version of the bible that would in time become what is known as the King James Authorized Version. He then gave them a list of fifteen instructions they had to use in the process. It was the third instruction that reveals his intent regarding the use of the word ekklesia. In his instructions, he wrote:

The old ecclesiastical words to be kept; as the word *church*, not to be translated *congregation*, &c.[4]

In other words, he specifically told them to use the word *church* instead of the correct translation of *ekklesia – assembly or congregation*. This constitutes a willful mistranslation of ekklesia.

The translators obeyed him without question except for the dilemma they faced in Acts 19. Take note of the following three verses.

Some therefore cried one thing, and some another: for the assembly was confused; and the more part knew not wherefore they were come together (Acts 19:32)

But if ye enquire any thing concerning other matters, it shall be determined in a lawful assembly (Acts 19:39)

---

[4] You can document this instruction by researching KING JAMES INSTRUCTIONS TO THE TRANSLATORS. This is the third of fifteen guidelines he gave them. http://www.kjvonly.org/other/kj_instructs.htm

And when he had thus spoken, he dismissed the assembly (Acts 19:41)

In all three of these passages, the word assembly was translated from the same word that Jesus used at Caesarea Philippi – ekklesia. The fact King James translators translated ekklesia correctly in these verses suggests that they knew the other 115 times ekklesia was being mistranslated. But why here? Why didn't they follow the mistranslation directive in this place as they did in all the other New Testament scripture? A careful read of these verses gives us a clue.

In Acts 19:32 it appeared the *assembly* was confused. If the word 'church' had been used rather than 'assembly' it would have suggested that a 'church' could at times be confused. The implication of this would probably not have gone over too well with King James. He considered himself to be the head of the church, his decisions were final, so confusion would not be acceptable. Thus, it was more apropos to suggest the *assembly*, not the *church* was confused.

Acts 19:39 actually defined one of the duties of the ekklesia, which is to make a determination on a given matter. However, the injection of the word 'lawful' posed a problem. The town clerk's recommendation to settle the matter in a *lawful assembly* implied that the gathering in Acts 19 was '*unlawful*'. Again, if the translators had used the mistranslated word 'church' it would suggest the possibility of an 'unlawful' church. Of course, for King James that would have been out of the question. So once again the translators made sure that it was an assembly, not a church that was unlawful.

## Ekklesia is not church in any form

14

Finally, in Acts 19:41 it states that the town clerk dismissed the *assembly*. In the context of this entire discourse, *the assembly* had been portrayed as confused and unlawful. Therefore, only a confused and unlawful assembly could have been dismissed. If the translators had continued to use the mistranslated word 'church', it would not have fit into the contextual narrative they presented.

Jesus said He would build an ekklesia. Ekklesia is not church in any form. The English word church is a deliberate mistranslation of what Jesus' said. It was inserted into scripture to support the ego and mindset of an ungodly monarch – King James. There is nothing inspired or divine about the use of the word church. It was deceptive and has been debilitating to the Body of Christ.

This willful mistranslation of ekklesia is the second reason why Jesus never said He would build a church.

# FACT 3: EKKLESIA AND CHURCH HAVE DIFFERENT MEANINGS AND HISTORIES

In the first chapter, you learned that the word church didn't exist in the first century and that it is pagan in its origin. In the second chapter, you learned that the English word 'church' was a willful mistranslation of the Greek word ekklesia. This chapter will give you the third reason we say that Jesus never said He would build a church. Ekklesia and church have two different meanings and histories.

Why did Jesus choose the word ekklesia?

To some He was viewed as a Rabbi. This religious title suggests there were other word choices He had that would have seemed to be more fitting (John 1:38, 49; 3:2).

First, Jesus could have said He would build His temple. The temple was the hub for all things relating to the Jews. From the wilderness when it was a moving tabernacle, to the glorious structure that was erected by Solomon, the temple represented Judaism at its core.

16

Jesus answered and said unto them, Destroy this temple, and in three days I will raise it up. Then said the Jews, Forty and six years was this temple in building, and wilt thou rear it up in three days? But he spake of the temple of his body. (John 2:19-21)

There was an incident when Jesus said that if the temple was destroyed, He would raise it up in three days. This statement drew ridicule from the religious leaders because they had no idea that He was referring to His body. Later, when the religious leaders were looking to crucify Jesus, they used His words to try and indict Him (Matthew 26:59-61; Mark 14:55-59).

In a private conversation with His disciples, He again prophesied that the temple would be destroyed. This time, He did not suggest that it would be rebuilt. It had become a weak shadow of its former glory. At Caesarea Philippi, even though the temple was the primary place that represented the Jews, Jesus did not say that He would build His version of it.

Jesus could have said He would build His synagogue. If you wanted to learn, discuss, or debate, the synagogue was the place to go. Jesus regularly taught in the synagogues, and scripture says that it was His custom to be there every Sabbath (Luke 4:15-16). If Jesus had said He would build His synagogue, surely it would have been an acceptable choice. He would have been potentially building a place to propagate His new religion. But again, this was not His choice at Caesarea Philippi.

After Peter declared that Jesus was the Christ, Son of the Living God, Jesus declared that upon that revelation He would build His ekklesia. Notice that Jesus did not take time to explain what an ekklesia was. That is because the disciples, and everyone else in understood the ekklesia.

Unlike the temple and the synagogue, the ekklesia in Jesus day, was not recognized as a Jewish or religious entity. It was secular, and that is why it is important to understand what the ekklesia was.


## DEFINING EKKLESIA

Ekklesia is the combination of two root words: ek meaning out from, and kaleo, which means to call.[1] It is easy to conclude that *ekklesia* simply means *to be called out.*

Words have basic definitions, but are at times, defined by culture. Remember, that words also create pictures in our mind. These pictures not only help us to understand the word, but also grasp its application.

In my book, *NO LONGER CHURCH AS USUAL,*[2] I wrote that the people in Jesus day understood the ekklesia to be an arm of the Roman government.[3] The Romans assimilated this concept into their culture from the Greeks. The ekklesia operated in public affairs long before the Romans decided to use it. Ekklesia clearly was not a religious term in those days.

It did not begin that way.

---

[1] https://www.ecclesia.org/truth/ekklesia.html

[2] NO LONGER CHURCH AS USUAL: *Restoring First Century Values and Structure to the 21st Century Church* Second Edition © 2013 T. Lemoss Kurtz

[3] Ibid Page 31 (at the time of publication, I equated ekklesia as being synonymous with church)

In the Old Testament, the Hebrew word qahal, was translated as ekklesia in the Septuagint, the Greek translation of Hebrew text. In English, it would commonly be translated as 'assembly'. It often referred to Israel being assembled before the Lord (Deuteronomy 4:10).

Daniel received a vision that spoke to the generation where Jesus would enter the earth.

> Thou, O king, sawest, and behold a great image. This great image, whose brightness was excellent, stood before thee; and the form thereof was terrible. This image's head was of fine gold [**Chaldean empire**], his breast and his arms of silver [**Medes-Persian empire**], his belly and his thighs of brass [**Grecian empire**], His legs of iron, his feet part of iron and part of clay [**Roman empire**]. Thou sawest till that a stone was cut out without hands [**the Kingdom of the Lord Jesus Christ**], which smote the image upon his feet that were of iron and clay, and brake them to pieces. Then was the iron, the clay, the brass, the silver, and the gold, broken to pieces together, and became like the chaff of the summer threshingfloors; and the wind carried them away, that no place was found for them: and the stone that smote the image became a great mountain, and filled the whole earth. (Daniel 2:31-35)

The scope of this book will not cover all the implications of Daniels vision, but I have inserted in brackets, certain empires that led to the time of Jesus Christ. You can see that Jesus was born during the time the known world was ruled by the Romans.

This leads us to a key historical factor regarding the ekklesia. The qahal/ekklesia, had undoubtedly survived conceptually throughout the generations from the Chaldeans to the Romans. The late Dr. Myles Monroe in his book, God's Big Idea, gives us greater insight of how ekklesia was understood in Jesus' time.

Whenever the Romans set up their government in a new territory, they sent a procurator, or governor, to rule the province in the name and authority of the emperor. At the time of Jesus' public ministry, Pontius Pilate was the procurator of Judea. In addition, the Romans borrowed many ideas of government from the Greeks, modified them, and made them their own. One of these was the idea of a "called-out assembly of citizens who met democratically over matters of common concern. This was, essentially, the structure of the Roman Senate. The Greek word for this assembly of citizens is ekklesia, which literally means "called-out ones." Both the word and the concept would have been familiar to the people of Jesus' day – the concept because they saw it in action regularly in everyday government, and the word because of its frequent appearance in the Septuagint, the Greek translation of the Old Testament that was in common use in Jesus' day, where it referred specifically to the children of God. [4]

Ekklesia had been practiced for hundreds of years. It was commonly understood by everyone. When the religious elite, government officials, or any average Joe on the street heard you mention the ekklesia, they understood it and its purpose. It wasn't simply a called-out assembly. It was much more than that.

When Jesus declared that He would build His ekklesia, He knew those around Him would understand the implications. These implications we will discuss in the next chapter.

## WHAT ABOUT CHURCH?

I will not repeat the pagan history of the word church, but I will give you another important historical aspect of our understanding of church.

---

[4] GOD'S BIG IDEA *Reclaiming God's Original Purpose for Your Life* © 2008 Myles Monroe Published by Destiny Image Publishers, Inc. Page 47

What do you think of when you hear the word 'church'? Usually when I asked this question, the first answer is a religious or dedicated building. It is defined as the place you go to every week. Others may mention their denomination, and some may suggest the idea that the 'church' are those who are called out. It's amazing that the last answer is the correct definition of ekklesia being applied to the wrong word.

Historically, from Pentecost to the third century, the early believers lived out their understanding of ekklesia. They gathered from house to house. There were no sacred places as it was thoroughly recognized that the collective body of believers were the dwelling place of the Lord.

The gathering from house to house in the first three centuries has been in plain sight scripturally, but it was obscured by the tradition of our practice of meeting in a dedicated building. How often have you consider the following passages, and their implications to you today?

> And they, continuing daily with one accord in the temple, and breaking bread from house to house, did eat their meat with gladness and singleness of heart (Acts 2:46)

> And daily in the temple, and in every house, they ceased not to teach and preach Jesus Christ (Acts 5:42)

> As for Saul, he made havock of the [ekklesia], entering into every house, and haling men and women committed [them] to prison (Acts 8:3)

> And Paul dwelt two whole years in his own hired house, and received all that came in unto him (Acts 28:30)

> The [ekklesia] of Asia salute you. Aquila and Priscilla salute you much in the Lord, with the [ekklesia] that is in their house (1 Corinthians 16:19)

> Salute the brethren which are in Laodicea, and Nymphas, and the [ekklesia] which is in his house (Colossians 4:15)

Whose mouths must be stopped, who subvert whole houses, teaching things which they ought not, for filthy lucre's sake (Titus 1:11)

And to [our] beloved Apphia, and Archippus our fellowsoldier, and to the [ekklesia] in thy house (Philemon1:2)

These are a minor sampling of the many obvious passages that reveal that believers gathered in homes. I have also inserted ekklesia in the places where it was incorrectly translated as church. This reveals that the ekklesia in the first century was a home-based movement.

## THE CONSTANTINE EFFECT

In the third century, Constantine made Christianity a state sanctioned religion. He embraced Christianity but never gave up his pagan beliefs. Most of his life, even after claiming to be a Christian, he was still considered the high priest of paganism with the title Pontifex Maximus, a title which later became the title for the Pope. He was a narcissistic egomaniac. Some therefor question the validity of his conversion.

Constantine began the erecting of buildings to house Christians. It is reported that some of the temples that had once been the meeting places for pagans were handed over to the Christians. The problem is that the Christians began to adopt many of the pagan practices. The pagan mindset became deeply intertwined with Christianity.

Gradually, over time the building became the primary symbol of Christianity. Implicit in the architecture was the level of sacredness that was being expressed by those who entered. The building has become so sacred that in some aspects it has become otherworldly.

Some believe that Constantine was somewhat of a hero. I don't agree with that assessment. The years of persecution endured by the first and second century believers came to an end because of him embracing Christianity.

Granted, no one likes being persecuted. But throughout the years, under such great pressure, Christianity continued to grow. Therefore, the Body of Christ grew from the blood of these first saints. Under Constantine's influence, the Body of Christ left the organic vibrancy of the home-based ekklesia to become the static dormant entity known as the church. It was as if satan decided that if you can't beat them, join them, make them comfortable, confuse their beliefs, and make them ineffective.

This history is important to understand. The ekklesia Jesus said He would build was never intended to be entombed behind the four walls of a building; neither was it to be help captive by man-made doctrine or pagan rituals.

When you understand the definition and history of ekklesia, you will also understand why Jesus would not declare that He would build such an entity as the church.

# FACT 4: EKKLESIA CONTINUES GOD'S ORIGINAL INTENT FOR MAN

Let us make man in our image – let them have dominion (Genesis 1:26-28). When God created man, He gave him clear instructions. Be fruitful, multiply, replenish the earth, subdue it and have dominion.

From the onset, it was God's original intent that man be His vice-regents in the earth. As long as man obeyed God, his capacity to manage the earth would be unlimited. Think about it. Every beast we know today is because God entrusted man to name them.

The devil, who had been evicted from the heavens, was now threatened in the earth by obedient mankind. As man followed God's mandate, the borders of his domain – the Garden of Eden – would expand. In time, the devil knew he would be evicted from the earth. So, he sought for a way to stop man.

Through deception, the devil tricked man into abdicating his role as God's representatives in the earth. Once again, the earth, in its entirety was under demonic control. But God had a plan.

> And the LORD God said unto the serpent, Because thou hast done this, thou art cursed above all cattle, and above every beast of the field; upon thy belly shalt thou go, and dust shalt thou eat all the days of thy life: And I will put enmity between thee and the woman, and between thy seed and her seed; it shall bruise thy head, and thou shalt bruise his heel. (Genesis 3:14-15)

The seed of the woman, Jesus Christ, would come and destroy the works of the devil (IJohn 3:8). In addition, He would restore man's authority to be the vice-regents of God in the earth (Matthew 24:14; 28:18-20; Acts 1:8).

During His earthly ministry, Jesus made several statements that show that God had not abandoned His original intent. Take note of these:

> Jesus answered and said unto them, Verily I say unto you, If ye have faith, and doubt not, ye shall not only do this which is done to the fig tree, but also if ye shall say unto this mountain, Be thou removed, and be thou cast into the sea; it shall be done. (Matthew 21:21)

> Go ye therefore, and teach all nations, baptizing them in the name of the Father, and of the Son, and of the Holy Ghost: Teaching them to observe all things whatsoever I have commanded you: and, lo, I am with you alway, even unto the end of the world. Amen (Matthew 28:19-20)

> And he said unto them, Go ye into all the world, and preach the gospel to every creature. He that believeth and is baptized shall be saved; but he that believeth not shall be damned. And these signs shall follow them that believe; In my name

shall they cast out devils; they shall speak with new tongues; They shall take up serpents; and if they drink any deadly thing, it shall not hurt them; they shall lay hands on the sick, and they shall recover. (Mark 16:15-18)

Behold, I give unto you power to tread on serpents and scorpions, and over all the power of the enemy: and nothing shall by any means hurt you. (Luke 10:19)

Verily, verily, I say unto you, He that believeth on me, the works that I do shall he do also; and greater works than these shall he do; because I go unto my Father. (John 14:12)

Jesus intended that all believers walk in Kingdom authority and power. His last instruction to His followers prior to ascending back to heaven was to go into Jerusalem and wait until they were given power through the infilling of the Holy Ghost. With this power, they would be witnesses in Jerusalem, Judea, Samaria and the world (Acts 1:8).

And I say also unto thee, That thou art Peter, and upon this rock I will build my [ekklesia]; and the gates of hell shall not prevail against it. (Matthew 16:18)

When Jesus announced that He would build His ekklesia, He immediately declared that the Gates of Hades would be powerless against it. This again shows that the ekklesia is not a group of people waiting for an escape from the earth. They are a collective body of believers who are empowered to fulfill the original Kingdom Mandate (Genesis 1:28).

The book of Acts is a record of the Apostles following Jesus commands. They healed the sick (Acts 5:15-16; 14:8-10), they raised the dead (Acts 20:9-12), and they cast out demons (Acts 16:16-18). They were in these ways, replicas of Jesus Christ. But it didn't stop there.

After being released from prison, apostles Peter and John gathered with a group of believers and shared all that had happened to them. They prayed that everyone in the room would be granted boldness, and that healing and signs and wonders would be done through them in the Name of Jesus. The result of this prayer was that everyone in the room were in fact filled and spoke the word with boldness (Acts 4:23-31).

I don't know if Stephen and Phillip were in the room when this took place, but later in Acts we see them doing the same miracles that were previously only done by the apostles (Acts 6:8; 8:5-7). This shows that the power of God to heal and deliver was available to all believers. Remember, signs follow believers (Mark 16:17).

The ekklesia consists of called out believers. What makes them unique is that they are all filled with the power of the Holy Spirit. I believe this is why Jesus confidently declared that the Gates of Hades, the source of demonic infiltration in the earth, cannot prevail against it.

Based on the historical evidence that the word church did not exist in Jesus day,

- that the word church is a willful mistranslation of ekklesia,
- that the word church and ekklesia have different definitions and histories, and,
- that ekklesia clearly continues God's original intent for man,

...this adds to the fact that Jesus would not have said that He would build a church.

Church was foundationally pagan and represented the opposite of the Lord's intent to send men and women filled with the Holy Spirit to recapture what the devil had stolen through deceit. But wait, there's more...

# Fact 5: JESUS GAVE THE KEYS OF THE KINGDOM TO HIS EKKLESIA – NOT THE CHURCH

It should be obvious to you at this point that Jesus could not or would not say He was building a church. By now you should understand that the original Greek word Jesus used to describe what He would build was ekklesia, not church. You should also have a basic understanding of the difference between the histories of ekklesia and church.

In these next three chapters we will look closely at the promises Jesus made only to His ekklesia. These will reinforce why Jesus did not say He would build a church.

## THE GATE OF HADES

The first thing Jesus said about the ekklesia, is that the Gates of Hades would not be able to prevail against it. This declaration reveals the impenetrable power that the ekklesia has. Whatever is born from God, overcomes the world – period (IJohn 5:4).

At Caesarea Philippi, there was a cave with a deep river flowing through it. In it, both human and animal sacrifices were made. This cave was known by the people in Jesus day as the Gate of Hades. To them, this place was the entrance to the underworld.

Hades was also thought to be among a trilogy of mythological gods that included Zeus and Poseidon. Zeus was the mythological god of the universe. Poseidon was the mythological god of the waters. And Hades was the mythological god of the underworld. He ruled over the abode of the dead. Each of these gods were believed to have powers that effected life on the earth.

> **Here is the reality. There is only one God, Elohim.**

Here is the reality. There is only one God, Elohim. He is the creator of both the heaven and the earth (Genesis 1:1; Psalms 8:3; 33:6). The earth, and everything in it belongs to Him (Psalms 24:1). The devil took control over the earth through deception and became known as the 'god of this world' (2Corinthians 4:4). It is only through deception that he exercises any control over the affairs of man in the earth. As believers, we are not to be ignorant of his tactics (2Corinthians 2:11).

When God declared that the heel of the woman's seed would crush the head of the serpent, it was clear that God's intent was to recapture everything stolen by the devil (Genesis 3:15). This was done through a series of divine legal maneuvers known as covenants. Through them God would empower man to reclaim stolen territory.

> But this shall be the covenant that I will make with the house of Israel; After those days, saith the LORD, *I WILL PUT MY LAW IN THEIR INWARD PARTS, AND WRITE IT IN THEIR HEARTS*; and will be their God, and they shall be my people. (Jeremiah 31:33)

> And *THOU SHALT LOVE THE LORD THY GOD WITH ALL THY HEART*, and with all thy soul, and with all thy mind, and with all thy strength: this is the first commandment. (Mark 12:30)

> That if thou shalt confess with thy mouth the Lord Jesus, *AND SHALT BELIEVE IN THINE HEART* that God hath raised him from the dead, thou shalt be saved. *FOR WITH THE HEART MAN BELIEVETH UNTO RIGHTEOUSNESS*; and with the mouth confession is made unto salvation. (Romans 10:9-10)

On the surface, you might conclude that it is solely the planet God is after. I would suggest that recovering the earth is a by-product of God's ultimate goal. His first desire is to recapture the heart of mankind. God has been in pursuit of man's heart from the day he rebelled in the Garden. Once man's heart has turned toward God, then recapturing and subduing the planet becomes an easy task (Zechariah 1:3; Malachi 3:7; 4:4-6). Godly men will care for the earth in a way that reflects the desire and design of the Father. Only hearts that are turned towards God can see the world and the earth from God's perspective.

## What in the World?

Sometimes our English words fail to convey the full thought behind a biblical text. We read a word in the bible and immediately define it by our western understanding. In the following passages, I will give you an overview of the Greek words that are often translated into English as earth and world.

The scope of this book will not cover in detail the Hebrew or Greek words from which the words earth and world are translated. That is a word study you should pursue on your own. However, a brief review of three specific Greek words and how they were used in biblical text, is necessary. In this, you will gain a greater appreciation for what Jesus has done for and provided to us.

The three Greek words that are often translated into English as 'world' are aion, oikoumene and kosmos. Aion (pronounced ahee-ohn), refers to an age or period of time; oikoumene (pronounced oy-kou-men'-ay) is similar to the Hebrew words that reference the land, and by implication the people in it as it implicitly referred to the Roman empire; and kosmos (pronounced kahs mos) refers to an orderly arrangement. Understanding the differences in these words will help you grasp the importance of the keys given to the ekklesia, and later as we will discuss, the authority to bind and loose.

The Greek word *oikoumene* is found fifteen times in the New Testament. Twelve times it is translated as world, and three times as earth. Each time it suggests the inhabited as well as the inhabitants of the earth. Read the following passages where *oikoumene* is used to get a glimpse of this word in context.

> And this gospel of the kingdom shall be preached in all the world [oikoumene] for a witness unto all nations; and then shall the end come. (Matthew 24:14)

> But I say, Have they not heard? Yes verily, their sound went into all the earth [ge], and their words unto the ends of the world [oikoumene]. (Romans 10:18)

> Because thou hast kept the word of my patience, I also will keep thee from the hour of temptation, which shall come upon all the world [oikoumene], to try them that dwell upon the earth [ge]. (Revelation 3:10)

In Romans 10:18 and Revelation 3:10, the English word *world* was translated from *oikoumene,* and the word *earth* was translated from a Greek word *ge.* The difference between *oikoumene* and *ge* is that *oikoumene* was limited to the known Roman empire, and *ge* referred to the entire globe.

## We read a word in the bible and immediately define it by our western understanding

The next word we will discuss is aion. This word is significant as it references a specific age or period of time.

> And lead us not into temptation, but deliver us from evil: For thine is the kingdom, and the power, and the glory, for ever (aion). Amen (Matthew 6:13).

Let's discover times when *aion* is translated as world. In my research, it was interesting for me to discover that the first time it is used, specifically in the King James version of the New Testament, is when

Jesus taught His disciples to pray. In Matthew 6:13 the words *'for ever'* are translated from the Greek word *aion*.[1]

This first use suggests an eternal dimension of aion. The kingdom of God is eternal, yet it manifests in every generation. Cultures, activities, and human authorities differ and change over time, but the kingdom of God remains constant. Daniel captures this juxtaposition of the eternal and the temporal when he wrote:

> How great are his signs! and how mighty are his wonders! his kingdom is an everlasting kingdom, and his dominion is from generation to generation. (Daniel 4:3)

As you continue reading, keep the eternal implications of *aion* in your mind. The day we live in differs from the days of our parents, but Jesus Christ and the power of His Kingdom does not change.

> Unto him be glory in the [ekklesia] by Christ Jesus throughout all ages (genos/generations), world (aion) without end (aion). Amen. (Ephesians 3:21)

Paul described satan as the 'god of this world (aion)'. Although the devil exists in the eternal sphere, he is by no means omnipresent. In each age he builds layers of deceptive ideas, cultural norms, false doctrines, and human governments that blind people from the glory of God. When we are born into the world, we are already surrounded by his deceptive influence. We unknowingly accept these as normal to our

---

[1] The closing phase "For thine is the kingdom, and the power , and the glory, for ever. Amen" is omitted in several other translations.

culture and are subsequently blinded to the debilitating impact they have on us.

Church is our norm – the concept of it was willfully slipped into the body of Christ in the 17th century by King James. This seemingly insignificant historical event has turned what Jesus intended from its original purpose.

> Teaching them to observe all things whatsoever I have commanded you: and, lo, I am with you alway, even unto the end of the world (aion). Amen. (Matthew 28:20)

When Jesus commissioned His disciples, He promised that He would be with them to the consummation of their age. Yet, this promise is timeless. This glorious promise applies to us in the day we live. He is also with us as we navigate through our time in the twenty-first century.

This eternal impact of ancient text is seen when Paul commanded the believers in Rome to not be conformed to this world (aion) (Romans 12:1-2). Followers of Christ in Rome had influences in their day that could easily draw them away from the good, acceptable and perfect will of God. We too must take heed to his admonition because of the seductive stimulus in our society.

The third Greek word we will consider is kosmos. This word refers to the orderly arrangement of the universe. It is how God structured and aligned the planets, but also the systems that govern them. The way gravity, the air we breathe, the way the earth turns on its axis and how it accurately travels around the sun all display the splendor of God's magnificent work.

Beyond these are spiritual structures that are unseen by the natural eye but are just as real as gravity and the air we breathe. The depth of this was revealed to me as I did a word study of one of my favorite scripture, John 3:16.

> For God so loved the world, that he gave his only begotten Son, that whosoever believeth in him should not perish, but have everlasting life.

When I discovered the 'world' that God gave His Son to die for, I have never been the same. Before I dug into it, I assumed the 'world' in the passage was the *oikoumene*. After all, it would be plausible that Jesus would go to Calvary to save mankind from their sin, and of course scripture does prove that to be a reality (Romans 5:8). We also know that salvation is more than a free ticket to heaven. We are brought out of darkness into His light to show forth His praises (1Peter 2:9). We are to walk as children of light (Ephesians 5:8). We are to go into this 'world' Christ died for and make disciples (Matthew 28:18-19; Mark 16:15).

According to John 3:16, the world God gave His Son for is the kosmos. He gave His Son to redeem the way He arranged things. If God gave His son for the way He arranged things, we need to clearly understand how things are organized?

From the beginning, God planted a garden with specific perimeters and placed man in it (Genesis 2:8-15). Man was created and commanded to be fruitful, to multiply, to fill or replenish the earth, and he was given the authority to subdue anything that opposed the purposes of God. Man would by divine nature walk in dominion (Genesis 1:26-28). Man would be God's vice-regents in all matters concerning the earth. Man lost his authority when he disobeyed God.

In the fulness of time, God sent His Son to redeem mankind (Galatians 4:4). Jesus came to destroy the works of the devil (Hebrews 2:14; IJohn 3:8). He came as the Lamb of God who would take away the sin of the world (kosmos). When He came into the world (kosmos), He was the final sacrifice (Hebrews 1:4-6).

John 3:16 declares that anyone who believes in Him will not perish, but they will have everlasting life. Jesus defined everlasting life as knowing God and the one He sent (John 17:1-3). It is to be rightly aligned with the Father's eternal intent, in this present age. This means that if you and I have eternal life, through Jesus Christ we are restored to the original intent of the Father which began when He said, "Be fruitful, multiply, replenish the earth and subdue it." In Christ, the dominion intended for man is restored. In Christ, we are now ambassadors sent to make disciples of nations and to reconcile the world (kosmos) back to God (Matthew 28:19; 2Corinthians 5:19-20).


ABOUT THOSE KEYS...

God would not give man an assignment without giving him the tools and authority to accomplish it. This brings us back to Caesarea

Philippi. After declaring that the gates of Hades would not prevail against it, Jesus promised the keys of the Kingdom to the ekklesia He would build.

> ...upon this rock I will build my [ekklesia]; and the gates of [hades] shall not prevail against it. And I will give unto thee the keys of the kingdom of heaven... (Matthew 16:18-19)

## KEY FACTORS

There are three things about keys you need to consider. First, when you give someone the keys to something, it implies a high level of trust. You would not give your keys to anyone you don't trust, or who would use them inappropriately. The keys Jesus promised to His ekklesia would give them access to the treasures of the Kingdom of Heaven.

Second, keys represent the right of access. Whoever has the keys, has access. Here are two examples that will help you understand this point.

In the Post Office I manage, many people have rented lock boxes or PO boxes to receive their mail. During the winter months, many of these postal customers go south. When they do, some of them leave the keys to their lock box with a friend or relative. Whoever that person is, has full access to the contents of the box. From time to time, a person without the proper key will request to retrieve the mail from a particular lock box. That person is denied simply because they do not have proof that they have a right to the contents of the box. Keys will unlock places that are denied to those who don't have them.

My son was the manager of a well-known retail outlet. In this role, He had keys to every area of the store he oversaw. Serving under him were assistant managers and supervisors who were called 'key-holders'. These employees were given a limited set of keys

> Keys will unlock places that are denied to those who don't have them

that allowed them to gain access to specific areas of the store in my son's absence. Unfortunately, there were at times those who violated their access and the trust they had been granted. Not only were they terminated, but all new locks had to be installed and everyone given a new set of keys. The reason for this was obvious. It was to restrict access to only those who had legitimate rights to access.

This leads us to the third aspect of keys. Keys activate specific locking systems. This may seem similar to the last point I made, but there is one critical difference. You must have the right key to activate a lock. My car keys won't unlock the door to enter my house. The key to my desk won't work in the lock to my office. This means that the keyholder must know where each key is designed to be used. Anyone who enters without the proper keys is most likely a thief (John 10:1).

Keys take on various shapes and forms. A key can be the little piece of metal we are most familiar with, but it can also be a combination like those used on a safe. In the digital age, keys can be a password, or series of numbers and letters that allow access into a particular computer program. Whatever the form, having the key proves the right to gain access.

Jesus said He would give the keys of the Kingdom of Heaven to His ekklesia – not the church. He placed His trust in His ekklesia.

## THE CHURCH SYSTEM HAS MISUSED THE KEYS...

The late Dr. Myles Monroe said, "When purpose is not known, abuse is inevitable." Failure to understand the purpose of the keys of the Kingdom has resulted in damage to the purpose of God, and the Body of Christ as a whole.

> At that time Berodachbaladan, the son of Baladan, king of Babylon, sent letters and a present unto Hezekiah: for he had heard that Hezekiah had been sick. And Hezekiah hearkened unto them, and shewed them all the house of his precious things, the silver, and the gold, and the spices, and the precious ointment, and all the house of his armour, and all that was found in his treasures: there was nothing in his house, nor in all his dominion, that Hezekiah shewed them not. Then came Isaiah the prophet unto king Hezekiah, and said unto him, What said these men? and from whence came they unto thee? And Hezekiah said, They are come from a far country, even from Babylon. And he said, What have they seen in thine house? And Hezekiah answered, All the things that are in mine house have they seen: there is nothing among my treasures that I have not shewed them. And Isaiah said unto Hezekiah, Hear the word of the LORD. Behold, the days come, that all that is in thine house, and that which thy fathers have laid up in store unto this day, shall be carried into Babylon: nothing shall be left, saith the LORD. (2 Kings 20:12-17)

Hezekiah made a grave error in revealing the treasures, the armor, and the money of Israel to the Babylonian king. It appears that Hezekiah exposed everything to him. This suggests that Hezekiah did not understand the value of what was in his possession. Isaiah the prophet declared that this act would result in everything in their treasures being carried away into Babylon. They would lose generations of treasures that his fathers had laid up.

The church system has done the same thing. It too has been careless with the treasures of the Kingdom. They exposed them by using them for self-gain, rather than for the purposes of the Lord. This has resulted in many of the principles of the Kingdom being stolen by New Age practitioners and self-help gurus.

> For what shall it profit a man, if he shall gain the whole world, and lose his own soul? (Mark 8:36)

Consider for a moment Mark 8:36, as well as Matthew 16:26 and Luke 9:25 as they all generally say the same thing. It is possible for a person to obtain great wealth and lose their most precious possession – their soul. This also reveals a truth about the value of what is in the Kingdom.

Many ungodly people have obtained worldly success by using principles from the Kingdom of Heaven. The problem is that they have effectively used the principles without acknowledging the King of the Kingdom. The principles work for whoever possesses and uses them correctly. But how did ungodly people gain access to treasures designed for the people of God? Just like Hezekiah, Kingdom principles in the hands of people with a church mindset, has resulted in a careless handling of these treasures. Let me give a few examples.

Meditation is a kingdom principle. It can infuse your spirit with the Word of God, the purposes of God, and the power of God (Joshua 1:8; Psalms 1:2; 77:12; 143:5; I Timothy 4:14-15). Other religions and New Agers have taken meditation and used it for self-gain, many times at the expense of others. Meditation has become so identified with New Ageism that believers shun it considering it as anti-god. The fact is that meditation is a biblical principle from the Kingdom.

Music is another example. I am a musician. I was trained as a classical pianist, but I enjoy nearly any genre I hear. Music styles often vary by culture and continent. Music from Latin America has a deep rich flavor that is completely different from the fun-loving sound of bluegrass songs. Jazz set's an atmosphere that is different from a philharmonic orchestra. People are drawn to the style the prefer. Gospel music took on a sound of its own.

Music which I believe was birthed in heaven, became corrupted by satanic influences. What should have been a tool of ministry, became attached to the perpetuation of ungodly lifestyles. Some music has specifically been written to conjure up demonic activity. This has resulted in believers rejecting various genres of music carte blanc, considering them ungodly. Rather than discern the spirit of the music, they reject the style.

Think about it. What style of music did David play that was powerful enough to drive evil spirits from Saul (1Samuel 6:23). What kind of music stirred the prophetic gift in Elisha? (2Kings 3:15). Who other than God determines what is an acceptable joyful noise? (Psalms 100:1-2). Is the use of various instruments proof of a certain genre of music? (Psalms 150:1-6).

My point is that once we grasp how valuable the treasures in the Kingdom are, we will handle the keys with utmost care. Jesus was specific about who He would give them to. We, the ekklesia must 'guard and keep' His treasures, and only access them for His purposes.

## CHURCH OR EKKLESIA

When you consider God's original intent, and the historical evidence of church, it becomes clear that Jesus would not build a 'church' and give it the keys allowing it full access to the Kingdom of Heaven. The church does not reflect His image or desire. It is too divided by ideology, doctrine and culture to be trusted with the keys. Such division makes it weak and ineffective (Matthew 12:25).

This does not suggest that believers in the church system are ungodly. Most are good people in a structure that was not sanctioned by heaven. Generally, they have a superficial understanding of the keys, as they have been taught from a church mindset rather than ekklesia perspective. Would Jesus give His keys to the church? I believe the answer is a resounding, "No!" Let's take this to the next level…

# FACT 6: ONLY THE EKKLESIA HAS THE AUTHORITY TO BIND AND LOOSE

After stating that He would build His ekklesia, Jesus first declaration was that the gates of Hades would not prevail against it. His ekklesia, consisting of men and women who have the revelation that He is the Christ, Son of the Living God, were promised the keys of the Kingdom of Heaven. The keys would be accompanied by the authority to bind and loose on earth, in sync with what is already bound and loosed in heaven.

Jesus only mentioned the ekklesia twice, and neither time did He explain what He meant. Why? Because ekklesia as a word and concept was thoroughly understood by His disciples, and all subsequent New Testament writers of that day. When Jesus used the ekklesia to describe what He would build, His choice of words also implied His intentions. The mistranslation of ekklesia to church has hidden this fact to most modern believers.

Like many words, ekklesia evolved in how it was used over the course of many years. It did not lose its basic meaning but shifted from referring to a gathering of the children of Israel, to being understood as a part of the Roman government. What began in the Old Testament with the Hebrew word qahal, continued in the New Testament as ekklesia.

> And when the people saw that Moses delayed to come down out of the mount, the people gathered themselves together [qahal] unto Aaron, and said unto him, Up, make us gods, which shall go before us; for as for this Moses, the man that brought us up out of the land of Egypt, we wot not what is become of him (Exodus 32:1).

> And Moses gathered [qahal] all the congregation of the children of Israel together [qahal], and said unto them, These are the words which the LORD hath commanded, that ye should do them. (Exodus 35:1)

Forty-seven times in the Old Testament, the Hebrew word qahal is used. Each time it refers to an assembly, a gathering, a convocation, or a coming together.

Every gathering had a purpose. For example, in Exodus 32:1, the people came together on their own to discuss a plan in response to the extended absence of Moses. In Exodus 35:1, Moses gathered the congregation together to give them the Word of the Lord. The pattern of

gathering *for a specific purpose* accompanies each use of qahal throughout the Old Testament.

It is this Hebrew word *qahal* that was later translated as *ekklesia*
in the Septuagint, which is the Greek translation of the Old Testament.
This suggests that ekklesia carries the same idea of *gathering for a specific purpose.*

The basic definition of ekklesia is derived from the combination
of two words. *Ek*, which means 'out from', and *kaleo*, meaning to call.
Together they generally mean 'to call out'. If you stop there, you will
miss the historical concept of ekklesia. Remember, in the Old Testament, qahal was more than just the gathering or coming together. It was
a coming together *for a specific purpose.* Likewise, ekklesia is not just
limited to being called out, it is to be called out *for a specific purpose.*
What is that purpose?

## THE EKKLESIA AND ROME

Jesus was born during the reign of the Roman empire. Rome was the
last in a succession of dynasties that had been prophesied by Daniel
(Daniel 2:31-45). The Romans picked up the concept of ekklesia, from
the Greeks and used it in the expansion of their rule. The governor of
each province of Rome appointed some who were called out to admin-
ister the policies of Rome throughout his territory. These called out
ones became the Roman ekklesia. Thus, people in Jesus day understood
the ekklesia to be an arm of the Roman government.

## The Authority of the Ekklesia

The Roman ekklesia was a ruling council that had clear authority given to it. They could legislate, confer or deny citizenship, establish policies and elect officials in behalf of the governor of the province. Ultimately, they carried out the policies of Rome. Don't miss this point. The Roman ekklesia had authority. They were in essence, a called out ruling council.

This abridged history of ekklesia will help you understand this next fact regarding the Lord's ekklesia. His ekklesia alone has been granted the authority to bind and loose in the earth in behalf of the Kingdom of Heaven. They are not just called out. The Lord's ekklesia is called out for a specific purpose. Like the Roman ekklesia represented the government of Rome, the Lord's ekklesia represents the government of the Kingdom of Heaven. They are called out and commissioned to implement the policies of the Kingdom of Heaven in the earth.

## Binding And Loosing

Jesus spoke of the ekklesia on two occasions. First, to declare His intent to build His own version of it, and the second time as an example of its authority. Let's look closely at the two times Jesus mentioned the ekklesia.

And I say also unto thee, That thou art Peter, and upon this rock I will build my [ekklesia]; and the gates of hell shall not prevail against it. (Matthew 16:18)

Jesus committed to giving the keys of the Kingdom to His ekklesia. With the keys, His ekklesia would be authorized to bind and loose. Binding and loosing became a clear indication of its authority. This was not to be an arbitrary binding and loosing, but rather there was to be a direct correlation between what was bound or loosed on earth, and what was bound or loosed in heaven.

When you read Matthew 16:19 in the King James version, it seems to say that heaven would agree with whatever we bound or loosed on earth. However, the opposite is true. The only things that can be bound and loosed on earth is that which heaven has first made the determination is needed. The Amplified Bible gives us a better understanding of this.

I will give you the keys of the kingdom; and whatever you bind (declare to be improper and unlawful) on earth must be what is ALREADY bound in heaven; and whatever you loose (declare lawful) on earth must be what is ALREADY loosed in heaven (Amplified Bible [words in caps for clarity])[1].

The adverb 'already' makes it clear that the ekklesia can only bind or loose what was previously bound or loosed in heaven. Other translations concur with this. The following is Matthew 16:19 in three other translations.

---

[1] *Matthew 16:19* THE AMPLIFIED BIBLE, EXPANDED EDITION Copyright © 1987 by The Zondervan Corporation and the Lockman Foundation

### The World English Bible[2]

I will give to you the keys of the Kingdom of Heaven, and whatever you bind on earth _will have been_ bound in heaven; and whatever you release on earth _will have been_ released in heaven."

### Charles B. Williams Translation[3]

...and whatever you forbid on earth _must be what is already forbidden in heaven_, and whatever you permit on earth _must be what is already permitted in heaven_.

### The New American Standard Bible[4]

...and whatever you shall bind on earth _shall have been bound in heaven_ and whatever you shall loose on earth _shall have been loosed in heaven_

Binding and loosing carries with it the idea of permitting or forbidding something to happen. It is to declare something as being lawful or unlawful. This is the level of authority Jesus has given to His ekklesia.

## TYPES AND SHADOWS

Many things in the Old Testament were in fact types and shadows of things that were existing in heaven. The priests, the tabernacle, the Ark of the Covenant, and the various sacrifices all foreshadowed the coming

---

[2] WORLD ENGLISH BIBLE Published 2000 Public Domain

[3] THE NEW TESTAMENT: _A Translation in the Language of the People_ by Charles B. Williams © 1937 by Bruce Humphries, Inc. Copyright © renewed 1965 by Edith S. Williams. MOODY BIBLE INSTITUTE

[4] _The New American Standard Bible, New Testament_ © 1960, 1962, 1963 by The Lockman Foundation

of, as well as the eternal existence of Jesus Christ (Hebrews 8:1-13). Jesus now sits on the right hand of the Father interceding and is the mediator of a better covenant (Romans 8:34; Hebrews 1:3; 12:2; 1Peter 3:22).

A deeper study of the Old Testament reveals numerous symbols that pointed to the coming of the Lord. The priest, the tabernacle, the sacrifices and much more carry aspects of the coming work of the Lords Kingdom in the earth. The great cloud of witnesses that lived prior to the birth of Christ, all knew something and someone greater was coming. They did not receive the promise during their lifetime (Hebrews 11:13-40; 12:1-3). That greater was the promise of the Messiah – Immanuel, God with us (Isaiah 7:14; Matthew 1:23).

The birth of Jesus Christ was more than just a child being born into the earth. His birth was entrance of the promised Son who would be given to re-establish the rule of God in the earth through man (Isaiah 9:6-7; Mark 16:17-18; John 14:12; Acts 1:8). He is the Son who would be given out of God's love for how He originally intended man to function with authority and dominion in the earth (Genesis 1:28; John 3:16 see Fact 5). He is the Son who would bring many sons into the earth (Hebrews 2:10; 1John 3:1-3; 4:17).

Jesus Christ is the Son who would declare that His ekklesia would be authorized to declare what was or wasn't permitted or lawful in the earth as determined by His Kingdom in heaven (Matthew 6:9-10; 16:19). At Caesarea Philippi, He made this clear for the first time.

Later, Jesus spoke of binding and loosing again. This time involved how to handle a local dispute.

> Moreover if thy brother shall trespass against thee, go and tell him his fault between thee and him alone: if he shall hear thee, thou hast gained thy brother. But if he will not hear thee, <u>then take with thee one or two more, that in the mouth of two or three witnesses</u> every word may be established. And if he shall neglect to hear them, tell it unto the [ekklesia]: but if he neglect to hear the [ekklesia], let him be unto thee as an heathen man and a publican. Verily I say unto you, <u>Whatsoever ye shall bind on earth shall be bound in heaven: and whatsoever ye shall loose on earth shall be loosed in heaven</u>. Again I say unto you, <u>That if two of you shall agree on earth</u> as touching any thing that they shall ask, it shall be done for them of my Father which is in heaven. <u>For where two or three are gathered together in my name, there am I in the midst of them</u>. (Matthew 18:15-20)

This passage is filled with powerful truths that reinforce the authority of the ekklesia to bind and loose. Once again Jesus used words and phrases that were clearly understood by the people in His day. For example, His mention of 'two or three witnesses' revealed the legal process to be used in this dispute. Let's look at this matter piece by piece.

First, if a brother offends another brother, the two of them should attempt to work out their differences alone. If they are unsuccessful, the offended brother should try to reconcile again in the presence of *two or three witnesses*.

The suggestion of *two or three witnesses* is more than having more ears to hear the matter. It implied the authority God had invested in believers. Remember Jesus lived during the time when the ekklesia was considered to be part of the Roman Empire. Within that understanding were other concepts; one was the idea of *two or three witnesses*. When two or three Roman citizens gathered anywhere in the world, they could be considered a *conventus*, short for *Conventus Civium Romanorum*.

## CONVETUS IRURIDICUS

Another term closely associated with *convetus* was the *conventus iruridicus*. The *conventus iuridicus* both provided the locations and created the administrative mechanism by which the Romans managed legal interactions and handled disputes between Roman citizens and the non-citizen inhabitants of the provinces. To have a conventus iruridicus in a territory was considered an honor.[5]

The two or three witnesses Jesus referenced could have been construed as a conventus iruridicus of the Kingdom where legal actions and disputes were to be handled. Thus, if the two or three – the Kingdom version of the conventus iruridicus – could not resolve the dispute, it was to be taken to the ekklesia.

The ekklesia became the final arbiter in the matter. Its decision would be final. If the offending brother did not accept the decision of the ekklesia, he would be considered a heathen or a publican, or an outcast from the Kingdom citizenry. One of the duties the Roman

---

[5] https://onlinel-brary.wiley.com/doi/abs/10.1002/9781444338386.wbeah26213

ekklesia had was the authorization to confer or deny citizenship. The Lord's ekklesia apparently has the same authority.

Jesus once again reminded the ekklesia that they had the right to bind and loose anything that had already been bound or loosed in heaven. The decision to deny a brother citizenship in the Kingdom was not a result of him not being liked by others, but rather the result of a clear judicial process outlined in the Kingdom of Heaven.

In the two instances where Jesus spoke of the ekklesia, Matthew 16:18-19 and Matthew 18:15-20, He invoked the authority it had to bind and loose. This is a level of authority only entrusted to His ekklesia — not the church. This sets up the final fact that shows us why Jesus never said He would build a church.

# FACT 7: ONLY BELIEVERS IN THE LORD'S EKKLESIA CAN REPRESENT THE KINGDOM OF HEAVEN

Let's do a brief recap of what we have discovered to this point. First, the word church did not exist in Jesus day. Jesus said He would build His ekklesia, which was commonly known as an arm of the Roman government.

Second, the English word church is a mistranslation of the Greek word ekklesia. The mistranslated word church was inserted into scripture by the orders of King James in the 17ᵗʰ century. He had this done on purpose in order to protect the hierarchal system he had in place to rule the 'church'.

Third, the words ekklesia and church have entirely different meanings and histories. Ekklesia as a concept began in the Old Testament with the Hebrew word qahal. Historically it involved those who gathered or came together for a specific purpose. The Septuagint translated qahal as ekklesia. It still refers to an assembly, but also carries the connotation of being called out for a specific purpose. Church on the other hand, has a more pagan history. Most of its background point to pagan origins.

Fourth, ekklesia re-establishes God's original intent for mankind to be God's vice-regents in the earth. It is those who are called out to be fruitful, multiply, replenish and subdue the earth with God-given dominion (Genesis 1:28). Fifth, Jesus was very clear that the keys of the Kingdom of Heaven would be given to His ekklesia. This suggest the access the ekklesia has to the treasures and strategies emanating from the Lord's kingdom. And six, the ekklesia alone was given clear authorization to bind and loose on earth what heaven declares needed to be bound or loosed.

Now we come to the seventh fact: only believers in the Lord's ekklesia can represent the Kingdom of Heaven. That should be a no-brainer. But, as we look around the religious landscape, we see all sorts of lifestyles claiming to be Christians.

## WHO ARE THE CHRISTIANS?

The term Christian has become so generic that anyone claiming to be one is generally accepted as such. Simply by adding an adjective to Christian suggests that the adjective is Christian. To challenge the adjective garners accusations of being judgmental. "Who are you to judge me?" This question attempts to protect a lifestyle that may run contrary to the Word of God.

Let's look at some of the adjectives we hear today. Adjectives such as Liberal, Conservative, Gay, Swinging, and Cursing divide the Body of Christ by acceptance of sin and social ideology. Denominational adjectives (i.e. Baptist, Methodists, Lutheran, Pentecostal, etc.) separate the Body of Christ through doctrinal stances. We allow adjectives like Black, White, Hispanic and the like to keep us comfortable in cultural and racial divisions. Even within these ideologies, doctrines and cultures there are deeper divisions making this topic far too complex to cover in this book. The point is that we are horribly divided.

To claim to be a Christian also carries with it the implication that the person is a believer. If you think about it for a moment, scripture speaks of those who follow Christ as believers – not Christians. The label of 'Christian' was given to the disciples in Antioch (Acts 4:26). This referred to someone who was a follower of Christ. King Agrippa, who in my opinion was being somewhat facetious, said that Paul almost persuaded him to be a Christian (Acts 26:28). Peter encouraged believers not to be ashamed if they endured suffering for being labeled a Christian (1Peter 4:16).

There are specific attributes resident in lives of believers. These will help you to discern the difference between a person carrying the label of being a Christian, and a true believer of the Lord Jesus Christ.

And these signs shall follow them that believe; In my name shall they cast out devils; they shall speak with new tongues; They shall take up serpents; and if they drink any deadly thing, it shall not hurt them; they shall lay hands on the sick, and they shall recover. (Mark 16:17-18)

Mark wrote that undeniable signs follow believers. Demons are cast out, new and supernatural tongues are spoken, serpents and poisons won't harm them, and the sick will be healed. The lack of these signs is not because the power of God has diminished, instead it exposes the reality that there is a lack of believers.

Jesus answered and said unto them, This is the work of God, that ye believe on him whom he hath sent. (John 6:29)

Through the Holy Spirit, we are empowered to do exactly what Jesus did in the earth. Scripture says that 'as He is — so are we' in this world'. The 'world' God gave Jesus to die for is the same world mentioned in IJohn 4:17. It is the kosmos — God's orderly arrangement of the universe. It is the world that responds to believers who walk in the authority they have been given (Genesis 1:28).

Behold, what manner of love the Father hath bestowed upon us, that we should be called the sons of God: therefore the world knoweth us not, because it knew him not. Beloved, now are we the sons of God, and it doth not yet appear what we shall be: but we know that, when he shall appear, we shall be like him; for we shall see him as he is. (IJohn 3:1-2)

But as many as received him, to them gave he power to become the sons of God, even to them that believe on his name: (John 1:12)

The greatest truth we should understand about believers is that they are empowered to become sons. Sonship is the highest level of recognition God gives to us. Jesus came to produce many sons – not a gender – but rather a spiritual designation given to men and women those who are led by the Spirit (Romans 8:14; Hebrews 2:10).

## RESTORING THE STANDARD FOR THE LORD'S EKKLESIA

You have learned in this book that in Jesus day, the ekklesia was known as an arm of the Roman government. They could legislate, confer or deny citizenship, establish policies, and when necessary, elect officials. Everything they did was in behalf of Rome.

Imagine the chaos that would have been created if Rome had entrusted this level of authority to anyone who was not loyal to their government? Yet, this is exactly what the church world has done. It has allowed individuals, who in some cases are practicing unbelievers, who are living openly in sin, to 'do the work of ministry'. This has made the Body of Christ look weak, anemic and confused.

> Jesus Christ would never entrust the Kingdom into the hands of nonbelievers

Jesus Christ would never entrust the Kingdom into the hands of nonbelievers. How do we determine who does or does not qualify? No doubt this will garner accusations of judgmentalism, legalism, closed mindedness, and your choice of phobias. But scripture cannot be ignored. Many will continue to be called, but still only a few will be chosen (Matthew 22:19).

In my book, LEAVING CHURCH BECOMING EKKLESIA, I wrote that we are coming into a 'Malachi-moment'. This is a season Malachi prophesied wherein those who returned to God would be empowered to discern between those who served Him and those who did not (Malachi 3:13-18). Jesus provided the litmus test for this determination.

> If any man come to me, and hate not his father, and mother, and wife, and children, and brethren, and sisters, yea, and his own life also, he cannot be my disciple. And whosoever doth not bear his cross, and come after me, cannot be my disciple. (Luke 14:26-27)

> So likewise, whosoever he be of you that forsaketh not all that he hath, he cannot be my disciple. (Luke 14:33)

In case this is not clear to you, here is another passage from the Amplified Bible that may help you.

> ...If any person wills to come after Me, let him deny himself [disown himself, forget, lose sight of himself and his own interests, refuse and give up himself] and take up his cross daily and follow Me [cleave steadfastly to Me, conform wholly to My example in living and, if need be, in dying also][1] (Luke 9:23)

The price for being a follower of Jesus Christ is high – and why shouldn't it be. He paid the ultimate price for us at Calvary. Therefore, He has the right to expect complete surrender from His followers. Unbelievers are not qualified to represent His Kingdom. Churches are

---

[1] THE AMPLIFIED BIBLE, EXPANDED EDITION Copyright © 1987 by The Zondervan Corporation and the Lockman Foundation

filled with people who follow ideological, denominational and cultural views, but are no where near being believers of the Lord Jesus Christ.

The spirit of compromise by Christians has crept into nearly every sphere of human existence. Music, politics, media, commerce, education, religion and even the family are not untouched. Too many Christians align themselves with fame, money and power under the guise of spreading the gospel. The line of demarcation is being drawn. Only believers, those disciples who give their all, will be found qualified to receive the keys of the Kingdom; be authorized to bind and loose; and have the right to represent the interest of the Kingdom of Heaven in the earth.

> To wit, that God was in Christ, reconciling the world unto himself, not imputing their trespasses unto them; and hath committed unto us the word of reconciliation. Now then we are ambassadors for Christ, as though God did beseech you by us: we pray you in Christ's stead, be ye reconciled to God. For he hath made him to be sin for us, who knew no sin; that we might be made the righteousness of God in him. (2Corinthians 5:19-21)

Only believers can represent the Kingdom of Heaven in the earth.

# What Does This Mean To You?

The purpose of this book has been to show that Jesus did not say He would build a church. You have seen this from a historical, etymological and of course scriptural evidence. But now you may be asking yourself, "What difference will this make in my life?"

Learning that Jesus did not say He would build a church may be unsettling for some. I personally wrestled with this for some time before discussing this subject publicly. When I did mention it to a few close friends, I was amazed that they already knew this fact, but had never pursued it at any depth. It wasn't until I understood the history behind both words that things began to change for me.

At the time I discovered this, I was in the process of writing a follow up to my book NO LONGER CHURCH AS USUAL. If you have read that book, you know that in it I explored the New Testament pattern of gathering from house to house. Throughout it I regularly referred to the 'house church'. I was familiar with the Greek word ekklesia, but I assumed that it was synonymous with the English word church. The follow-up book I was attempting to write was to show how to transition from the traditional 'church' into regional networks of 'house churches'.

I struggled with what to write. In my spirit it felt that something was missing. If I had ignored what I was sensing and continued down the path that ekklesia and church were the same, my follow up book would have been no more than a treatise on leaving the church sanctuary for a living room – with no significant purpose. As I retraced the difference between ekklesia and church, the Lord's intent for you and I became more evident. The difference is profound. Even more, the effect each word has on the Body of Christ is tangible. This final chapter will show why understanding the difference between ekklesia and church is vitally important to you as a believer.

## ALL WE HAVE EVER KNOWN IS CHURCH

If you are like most people reading this book, you are very familiar with 'church'. Nearly every community is peppered with 'church buildings'. Every weekend, millions of people get up to 'go to church'. People pride themselves with identifying with a particular 'denominational church'. Church programs, church events, and church missions are deeply engrained into our psyche. Because 'church' is all we have known, the reality of ekklesia has been hidden, unconsidered and insignificant.

No one would deny the good things that has been done through the 'church' over the years. Millions of people have been saved, delivered and set free in the 'church as we know it'. So, what's the problem? Simply put, church is not what Jesus intended to build. I heard an analogy that helps to shed some light on this issue.

Imagine that you hired a caterer to prepare a meal for a banquet. You explained that you wanted prime rib, sautéed broccoli, twice-baked potatoes, and strawberry cheesecake for the desserts. On the day of the banquet, you arrive to find the caterer setting up an elaborate meal of baked salmon, rice pilaf, brazed carrots and chocolate mousse for dessert. Regardless of how good the salmon entre' was – it was not what you ordered. The salmon entre' could even be the chefs signature meal, known around the world as an award-winning dish – but it is not what you ordered. Regardless as to how succulent and appetizing it may be – it is not what you ordered.

Church is not what Jesus ordered. All the good it has done and may continue to do can not overcome the fact that Jesus said He would build His ekklesia, not His church. Ekklesia and church are entirely two different entities. The difference between what Jesus said – ekklesia – and what we have become – church – is dramatic and life changing.

## THE ORIGINAL INTENT

Let's look again at God's intent for man from the beginning. Man was created in the image and likeness of God to serve as His representatives in the earth. Man was commanded to be fruitful, to multiply, to replenish the earth and subdue it. By divine edict, man would walk the earth in dominion (Genesis 1:26-28). When man disobeyed God regarding the Tree of Life, God's intent was disrupted, but He was not dissuaded. He set in motion a plan to restore man back to his original position (Genesis 3:15).

Through a series of seven covenants[1], culminating with the covenant we currently have in Jesus Christ, God re-established man as His vice-regents in the earth (Matthew 28:19; Mark 16:15-20; Acts 1:8). During His earthly ministry, Jesus declared that He would build His ekklesia, and the gates of hades would not be able to prevail over it.

Remember that the ekklesia was modeled after the Roman ekklesia. It had power to legislate, confer or deny citizenship, set policies, and elect officials in behalf of the Roman government. Likewise, the Lord's ekklesia would do the exact same thing as representatives of the Kingdom of Heaven.

The devil, who deceived man in the Garden of Eden, was again being overcome by men and women filled with the power of the Holy

---

[1] The Edenic Covenant, The Adamic Covenant, The Noahic Covenant, The Mosaic Covenant, The Abrahamic Covenant, The Davidic Covenant, The Covenant in Christ Jesus each detailed in the book THE SEVEN COVENANTS *A Study of The Bible Through The Seven Great Covenants of The Scriptures* by Charles Gilbert Weston © 1990 Apostolic Missions Foundation Weston Bible Ministries

Spirit (Luke 10:17; John 14:12). At first, he tried to destroy the Body of Christ with intense persecution. But the more he persecuted them, they increased even more (Acts 8:1; 11:19; 12:1, 24; 19:20).

In the fourth century, the devil used another tactic. We could describe it by the old axiom, "If you can't beat them — join them." Through Constantine an edict was given that essentially reversed the persecution against Christians. Christianity became a state sanctioned religion. Because of Constantine's beliefs in other gods, paganism was infused and masked as Christian rituals. The gatherings from house to house were replaced by meetings in ornate buildings decorated with pagan symbolism.

For the next 1,200 years, Christianity as a religion fell deeper and deeper into superstition and paganism. Phrases like *kuriakê oikia* and words like circe, drawn from paganism, became part of the language. You may recall from the first chapter that these were early forms of the word 'church'. Then, early in the sixteenth century a German monk, Martin Luther, challenged the 'church's' authority. He posted his now famous 95 Thesis on the door of the Wittenberg Castle giving birth to the Protestant Reformation. God began to restore critical truths to the Body of Christ.

In 1611, satan countered with more disruption. King James commissioned his translation of the bible. In it, as you have previously learned, he had the Greek word ekklesia purposely mistranslated as the English word church. You may wonder why we are repeating this historical fact throughout this book. It is because these factors play a significant part in understanding the impact the switch from ekklesia to church has had on you, and the Body of Christ as a whole.

## IDENTITY THEFT

The shift from ekklesia to church literally engrained a change in the identity of the body of Christ. Because the simplicity of the house to house gatherings had been replaced by the sterile atmosphere of the dedicated building, people were ripe for this change in mindset.

The switch literally helped to solidify how 'Christians' viewed themselves. A change in identity creates a change in activity. It creates a different view of one's purpose. It creates a different view of expectations. Yes, in recent years there have been some teaching regarding the various ministry gifts, but they have been pigeon holed into a system that did not exist in the first century. There has been teaching regarding the authority of the believer, but it was still encased in a system foreign to divine intent.

How you see yourself is critical to what you do. As we summarize this book, let's look at some of the changes precipitated by changing ekklesia to church. The following are three of these changes.

## MEMBER OR CITIZEN?

One such effect has been the advent of 'church membership'. Scripture never suggests that we are members of an organization.

We are distinct members of the Body of Christ (Romans 12:5; I Corinthians 12:12, 27). The body is organic, yet each part has a specific function (Romans 12:4; Ephesians 4:16). Even when scripture refers to the 'household of faith' (Galatians 6:10) and the 'household of God' (Ephesians 2:19), it was not to suggest an institutional group with members, but rather a body of believers similar to a family. The Nelson's Illustrated Bible Dictionary states,

> *Household* is also used in a spiritual or symbolic sense. United by God's election and salvation through Jesus Christ, Christians are included in God's household of faith.[2]

Today, you hear the terms 'body' and 'household' in conjunction with a church organization. Church membership has become so pervasive that in some cases it is equated to salvation. This concept is no different from the 'Edict of Toleration' that ended persecution against Christians but set it up as a state religion where mere membership in the 'Christian class' was enough. It was like joining a political party. Simple membership replaced accepting Jesus Christ.

Biblical membership refers to each member functioning in their specific place. Church membership refers to different status classes – clergy or laity. Hierarchal class distinctions do not exist in the Kingdom of God. Biblical membership builds the entire body and each member within it. Church membership advances the causes of the organization, too often at the expense of some of the members. Biblical members

---

[2] Page 496 'household' NELSON'S ILLUSTRATED BIBLE DICTIONARY Copyright © 1986 Thomas Nelson Publishers

draw strength from the 'oneness' they have with Christ and other believers. Church member accentuate their doctrinal, ideological and cultural differences they have with other churches. When Jesus said He would build His ekklesia, He did not have the church divisive mindset.

## PARTICIPANT TO SPECTATOR

The advent of the church system took believers out of the primary gatherings from house to house and corralled them in dedicated buildings. Slowly believers stopped being participants in the purposes of God and became spectators in an auditorium. The practice of thinking and dialoguing was replaced by listening and accepting religious dogma. Rather than pursuing and functioning in purposes designed by the Holy Spirit, believers now sit silently and wait for task designed to build the church organization.

## HIERARCHY

One of the reasons King James wanted the word church used, was to protect the control he had over the church. He was the self-appointed head of the Church of England and he ruled it through bishops he appointed. His church system was patterned after secular governmental hierarchy.

In a hierarchal system, leaders' rule from the top down. In the Kingdom, leaders serve from the bottom up. In the Kingdom, leaders serve each member of the Body of Christ as they pursue their calling, purpose and ministry.

The Lord's ekklesia has leaders within it. They are functional rather than hierarchal. Each person serving in a function is on equal footing with all other believers. Their function simply describes how they serve the Body of Christ. Paul articulated this clearly.

> ... neither he who plants is anything, nor he who waters, but God who gives the increase. Now he who plants and he who waters are one, and each one will receive his own reward according to his own labor. For we are God's fellow workers; you are God's field, you are God's building. According to the grace of God which was given to me, as a wise master builder I have laid the foundation, and another builds on it. But let each one take heed how he builds on it. For no other foundation can anyone lay than that which is laid, which is Jesus Christ. (1Corinthians 3:7-11 New King James Version)

## DON'T BLAME CHURCH FOLKS

Learning something new is exciting, but it is also a privilege. It is not an opportunity to prove you are better than someone else. Unfortunately, there are some who misuse fresh insights as a weapon to belittle and demean others. I want to be abundantly clear, learning about ekklesia does not make someone superior to another.

Facebook has spawned a new breed of self-proclaimed guardians of truth who seem to feel it is their right to attack those who have not embraced some new insight. These 'spiritual watchdogs' pride themselves in pointing out the flaws in everyone else. Social media has embolden some who consider themselves 'prophets of correction'. They are highly critical of those who don't have their 'present revelation'. Their vitriolic approach too often has a following of people who seem to feel their beliefs are superior to all others.

I recently saw a post by one such person who justified their harshness by likening it to the Old Testament prophets that rebuked kings and the wrong-doings of Israel. Such rebuke is totally out of context when it comes to receiving a new revelation. As we discover more about ekklesia, I implore you to handle this truth with reverence. Our role is simply to share this with as many believers we can. Allow the Holy Spirit to reveal this truth to God's people.

Church is all most of us have ever known. Ekklesia is new to many, even though the facts have been available for centuries. Across this country, and around the world believers are awakening to the fact that Jesus never said He would build a church. The Holy Spirit is releasing this truth to empower the Body of Christ. He is bringing this truth to the forefront – not us. Our role is to share what has been revealed to us, and then allow Him to open the eyes of believers (I Corinthians 15:3; Galatians 1:12).

This is a critical time for God's people. He is poised to release millions of believers into the earth to do great Kingdom exploits. Jesus is activating His ekklesia. He is calling out those who have the revelation that He is the Christ, Son of the Living God. His fully functioning ekklesia will wreak havoc on the Gates of Hades (Matthew 16:18-20).

God entrusts revelation to us. We must handle it with reverence and respect. To receive something fresh from the Throne of God is a privilege, not a right. Treat everything you learn about ekklesia with honor. Pray for those who don't see, or that may even reject this truth. Be an example of what you believe. Demonstrate the truth you know. It is hard for people to reject activated truth (Acts 4:16).

## What Happens Next?

We are entering The Day of the Saints. Since the reformation of the 17th century, there has been a progressive restoration of biblical truths with the most recent being that of the five-fold ministry gifts. Unfortunately, as these truths were restored, people camped on some of them giving rise to sectarian and denominational groups. Even with the five-fold ministry gifts, religious groups have taken on labels of being apostolic, prophetic and the like. Embracing the label without embracing the purpose perpetuates the divisive pattern seen in church systems. Therefore, it is critical that we look at the specific purpose of the ministry gifts Jesus gave.

> And he gave some, apostles; and some, prophets; and some, evangelists; and some, pastors and teachers; For the perfecting of the saints, for the work of the ministry, for the edifying of the body of Christ: (Ephesians 4:11-12)
>
> … in order to equip the saints for the work of serving, for the building up of the Body of Christ-- (Ephesians 4:12 Montgomery New Testament)
>
> …. to prepare God's people for works of service, so that the body of Christ may be built up (Ephesians 4:12 New International Version)

…. His intention was the perfecting and the full equipping of the saints (His consecrated people), [that they should do] the work of ministering toward building up Christ Body (the church ekklesia) (Ephesians 4:12) [authors correction of church to ekklesia]

As you read Ephesians 4:11 and specifically verse 12, it is clear that the Lord's purpose was to equip and train the saints so that they could do the work of ministry. It has been the Lord's original intent from the beginning to release you to fulfill your calling, purpose and ministry. When millions of believers like you are trained and equipped and ultimately released by the five-fold ministry gifts, the dynamic of church as we know it will change. As millions of believers like you pursue their God-given assignments, religious structures will be forced to adjust to the original intent of the Father.

We are entering a time of transition. This is a season for you to take specific steps to enjoy the present truth being released. The following are four areas that are important for you to consider as we close this book.

1. PRAY. Seek the Lord to understand this shift. Ask the Lord to reveal to you the truth about ekklesia and specifically what it means to you. Prayer is the key to everything you receive from the Lord.

2. PURSUE YOUR PURPOSE. If you don't feel confident in pursuing your purpose, it could mean that you have not been adequately equipped. Spend time discovering what your

assignment is in the earth. As you do, trust God to surround you with ministry gifts that will equip you to succeed.

3. **PREPARE YOURSELF.** I have a statement that I share with my leaders, "The more you know — the more you grow". This book is not the whole story. I pray it has stirred you to pursue more. I encourage you to do more research and study. There are resources included at the back of this book that can aid you.

4. **POSITION YOURSELF.** If this book has served to open your eyes to the truth regarding ekklesia, I trust that the Lord will connect you with others pursuing this in your area. No. This is not advocating for you to leave your 'church'. Transition does not suggest walking away without explicit direction of the Holy Spirit. To position yourself means to align with others of like mind who are praying, pursuing and preparing themselves to be in the purposes of God in this season.

Jesus never said He would build a church. He explicitly declared that He would build His ekklesia. Hades gates would not be able to prevail against it. He would entrust His ekklesia with the keys of the Kingdom of Heaven. His ekklesia is authorized to bind and loose on earth what Heaven had determined needed to be bound and loosed (Matthew 16:18-20).

God is calling out believers like you to impact the earth. If you are a believer, this is your day. This is your season. Are you ready to experience what God intended for you from the very beginning? If so, get ready for an exciting journey. Your best is before you...

# SUGGESTED RESOURCES

EKKLESIA RISING: *The Authority of Christ in Communities of Contending Prayer* © 2014 by Dean Briggs Published by Champion Press Page 108

EKKLESIA: *The Government of the Kingdom of Heaven on Earth* ©2014 Joe Nicola Published by Spring Mill Publishing

BEYOND CHURCH: *An invitation to experience the lost word of the bible* © 2015 Steve Simms Published by Harper Simms Press

THE EKKLESIA: *The church that Jesus is building* © 2012 Anthony Daley Published by Creation House

EKKLESIA: *Rediscovering God's Instrument for Global Transformation* © 2017, 2017 by Ed Silvoso Published by Chosen Books

# BOOKS BY THE AUTHOR

LEAVING CHURCH BECOMING EKKLESIA: *Because Jesus never said He would build a church* ©2017 T. Lemoss Kurtz Published by Kingdom Word Publications

THE BELIEVERS GUIDE FOR LEAVING CHURCH BECOMING EKKLESIA ©2017 by T. Lemoss Kurtz Published by Kingdom Word Publications

NO LONGER CHURCH AS USUAL *Restoring first century values and structure to the 21st Century Church* Second Edition © 2013 by T. Lemoss Kurtz Published by Kingdom Word Publications

ONLINE REFERENCES ARE ACTIVE AS OF THE DATE OF PUBLICATION

http://www.greatsite.com/timeline-english-bible-history/king-james.html

https://gotquestions.org/Bishops-Bible.html

https://www.britannica.com/topic/divine-right-of-kings

http://www.wwnorton.com/college/history/ralph/workbook/ralprs20.htm

https://www.bl.uk/collection-items/the-true-law-of-free-monarchies-by-king-james-vi-and-i

https://www.ecclesia.org/truth/ekklesia.html

http://www.kjvonly.org/other/kj_instructs.htm

http://sidroth.org/articles/church-isnt-new-testament/

## OTHER BOOKS

THE SPONTANEOUS EXPANSION OF THE CHURCH: *and the Causes Which Hinder It* by Roland Allen. First Published 1927 Public Domain

CHURCH REFUGEES: *Sociologists reveal why people are DONE with the church but not their faith* © 2015 Josh Packard and Ashleigh Hope Published by group.com

MISSIONARY METHODS: *St Paul's or Ours?* By Roland Allen © 1962, World Dominion Press

PAGAN CHRISTIANITY? *Exploring the Roots of Our Church Practices* © 2002, 2008 by Frank Viola and George Barna Published by Tyndale. First printing by Present Testimony Ministry in 2002

www.ingramcontent.com/pod-product-compliance
Lightning Source LLC
Chambersburg PA
CBHW071102040426
42443CB00013B/3373